# How to do Product Marketing Well

## Practical Guide

G. Dellis

Copyright © 2024

# Guide to Product Marketing

# 1.Introduction

Product Marketing is a strategic business function that focuses on the positioning, promotion, and selling of a product in the market. Its primary goal is to ensure that the product meets customer needs and stands out from the competition. Product marketing activities include market research, developing marketing strategies, launching new products, and monitoring sales performance.

The main responsibilities of product marketing include:

1. **Market Research**: Collecting and analyzing data on consumer needs, market trends, and competition to inform product development and marketing decisions.

2. **Positioning Definition**: Establishing the product's position in the market by

identifying its unique strengths and key messages that differentiate it from competitors.

3. **Launch Strategy**: Planning and managing the product launch, ensuring all involved departments (development, sales, marketing) are aligned and ready to support the launch.

4. **Product Promotion**: Developing marketing campaigns that communicate the product's value to potential customers through various channels (advertising, social media, PR, etc.).

5. **Market Education**: Creating educational content, such as white papers, webinars, and demos, to help customers understand how the product solves their problems.

6. **Performance Analysis**: Monitoring and

analyzing sales and product performance, collecting feedback to continuously improve the product and marketing strategies.

#### Importance of Product Marketing

Product marketing is crucial for the success of a product and, consequently, for the overall success of the company. Its main importances include:

1. **Product-Market Alignment**: Ensures that the product meets market and customer needs, reducing the risk of failure. Without a thorough understanding of the market, a product may not meet the real needs of consumers.

2. **Competitive Differentiation**: Helps position the product uniquely, highlighting its advantages over competitors. This is essential in saturated markets where customers have many options to choose from.

3. **Efficient Launch**: A well-orchestrated product launch can make the difference between a product that fails and one that succeeds. Product marketing ensures that all stakeholders are coordinated and that the product is introduced to the market in the most effective way possible.

4. **Optimized Marketing Resource Utilization**: Helps focus marketing efforts on the most effective messages and channels, optimizing the ROI (return on investment) of marketing campaigns.

5. **Sales Support**: Provides the sales team with the tools and information they need to sell the product effectively, including sales materials, training, and market data.

6. **Continuous Feedback and Improvement**: Collects feedback from customers and sales performance to make continuous improvements to the product and

marketing strategies. This feedback cycle is vital for maintaining the product's relevance over time.


Product marketing is a fundamental function that connects the product to customers, ensuring that the solutions offered by the company align with market needs and that the product has the best possible impact on the target audience.

## 2. Identifying the Target Market

Identifying the target market is a crucial step in the marketing process. This process allows companies to focus their resources on the most promising market segments, thus increasing the chances of success for their marketing strategies. Identifying the target market means understanding who the potential customers are, their needs, preferences, and purchasing behaviors. Here's how to do it:

#### 1. Collecting Demographic Data

Demographic data provides an overview of potential customers based on criteria such as age, gender, income, education level, marital status, and occupation. This information can be collected through:

- **Surveys and Questionnaires:** Effective tools for gathering specific data directly from potential customers.

- **Analysis of Existing Data:** Utilizing data from internal sources (customer databases, CRM) and external sources (market studies, public statistics).

#### 2. Market Segmentation

Once demographic data is collected, the next step is to segment the market into homogeneous groups. Segmentation can be based on various criteria:

- **Geographic:** Division of the market based on regions, cities, or specific neighborhoods.

- **Demographic:** Based on age, gender, income, education, occupation, marital status.

- **Psychographic:** Considers psychological aspects of consumers, such as values, interests, lifestyles, personality.

- **Behavioral:** Based on consumer behaviors, such as purchasing habits, product usage, brand loyalty.

#### 3. Analyzing Consumer Needs and Preferences

Understanding consumer needs and preferences is fundamental. This can be achieved through:

- **Focus Groups:** Small groups of people discussing the product or service, providing direct feedback.

- **Interviews:** In-depth conversations with potential customers to understand their needs and expectations.

- **Observation:** Studying consumer behavior in natural environments, such as stores or online.

#### 4. Competitor Analysis

Analyzing competitors can provide valuable

insights into the target market. By studying their customers, marketing strategies, and strengths/weaknesses, it is possible to identify areas of opportunity. This analysis can include:

- **Benchmarking:** Comparing your performance with that of competitors.

- **Mystery Shopping:** Direct experience of the services offered by competitors.

- **Feedback Analysis:** Monitoring reviews and feedback on competitors' products.

#### 5. Creating Buyer Personas

Buyer personas are detailed representations of ideal customers. These personas include demographic, psychographic, behavioral data, and purchasing motivations. Creating personas helps visualize and better understand the target market.

#### 6. Market Testing

Before launching a product on a large scale, it is useful to test the market with a pilot product or a limited marketing campaign. This allows for feedback collection and strategy refinement.

#### 7. Using Data Analysis Technologies

Data analysis tools, such as Google Analytics, CRM, and marketing automation platforms, can provide insights into the online behaviors of potential customers. These tools help monitor customer interactions with the website, email campaigns, and social media.

### Analyzing the Competition

Competition analysis is a strategic process that allows companies to better understand the market in which they operate and identify opportunities and threats from competitors. This process involves various phases and techniques for collecting and analyzing information on competitors.

#### 1. Identifying Main Competitors

The first step is to identify who the main competitors are. These can be direct (offering similar products or services) or indirect (offering alternative solutions to customer needs). Sources for identifying competitors include:

- **Market Research:** Industry studies, market reports, and sector analysis.

- **Search Engine Analysis:** Searching for relevant keywords in your sector to see which companies appear in search results.

- **Direct Observation:** Visits to physical stores and analysis of competitors' websites.

#### 2. Collecting Information on Competitors

Gathering detailed information on competitors is essential for in-depth understanding. Information can be collected from:

- **Competitors' Websites:** Examining content, offers, pricing strategies, and promotions.

- **Social Media:** Analyzing presence and activity on social media, including posts, customer interactions, and reviews.

- **Customer Reviews:** Reading customer reviews on platforms like Google, Yelp, and Amazon to understand perceived strengths and weaknesses.

- **Industry Publications:** Studies and reports published by trade associations, research companies, and consultancy firms.

#### 3. SWOT Analysis of Competitors

A SWOT analysis (Strengths, Weaknesses, Opportunities, Threats) helps evaluate competitors' strengths, weaknesses, opportunities, and threats. This approach provides a clear view of areas where competitors excel and areas where they could improve.

#### 4. Analyzing Marketing Strategies

Understanding competitors' marketing strategies is fundamental. This includes the analysis of:

- **Key Messages:** What messages and value propositions they are communicating to customers.

- **Marketing Channels:** Which channels they use to reach customers (social media, email marketing, online advertising, etc.).

- **Promotions and Special Offers:** What types of promotions and discounts they offer.

- **Marketing Content:** Quality and type of content they produce (blogs, videos, infographics, etc.).

#### 5. Benchmarking

Benchmarking involves comparing your performance with that of main competitors. This can include metrics such as:

- **Market Share:** Percentage of the market held by competitors compared to your own.

- **Revenue and Growth:** Financial data and growth rates.

- **Customer Engagement:** Measurement of engagement on social media, conversion rates, and customer retention.

#### 6. Mystery Shopping

Mystery shopping involves an anonymous

person making a purchase from a competitor to evaluate the quality of service, customer experience, and product quality. This method provides a direct and unfiltered perspective of competitors' operations.

#### 7. Price Analysis

Comparing competitors' product or service prices is essential for understanding their market positioning. This analysis can reveal opportunities to adjust your prices and improve competitiveness.

#### 8. Product Innovation and Development

Monitoring competitors' research and development activities can provide indications of emerging trends and future product innovations. Sources of information include patents, press releases, and new product announcements.

#### 9. Distribution Channel Analysis

Understanding how competitors distribute their products can reveal opportunities to improve your distribution strategy. This can include the evaluation of online and offline channels, partnerships with distributors, and logistics.

#### 10. Using Monitoring Technologies

Technological tools such as competitive analysis software, social media monitoring platforms, and market intelligence systems can automate the collection and analysis of information on competitors. These tools help maintain a constant flow of up-to-date and relevant data.

Identifying the target markct and analyzing the competition are interconnected and fundamental processes for the success of any marketing strategy. A thorough understanding of your audience and competitors' movements allows companies to develop more competitive offerings, improve their marketing strategies, and effectively position themselves in the market. With a systematic and thorough approach, companies can leverage this information to make informed and strategic decisions, ensuring sustainable growth and a lasting competitive advantage.

# 3. Define Product Objectives in Product Marketing

Defining product objectives is a crucial phase in product marketing. These objectives serve as a guide for the development, launch, and growth of the product in the market. Well-defined objectives help ensure that all marketing and development activities are aligned and oriented towards achieving the desired results. Below, we will explore in detail how to define product objectives, the types of objectives to consider, and the methodologies for measuring and achieving them.

### 1. Importance of Defining Objectives

#### A. Strategic Alignment

Product objectives must be aligned with the company's vision, mission, and strategic goals. This ensures that all teams work towards a common purpose, facilitating collaboration and improving operational efficiency.

#### B. Focus and Prioritization

Clear objectives help concentrate resources on key activities that significantly impact the product's success. This prevents resource dispersion and allows for the prioritization of the most important initiatives.

#### C. Performance Measurement

Defining specific and measurable objectives allows for an objective evaluation of the product's performance. This helps identify areas for improvement and make data-driven decisions.

### 2. Types of Product Objectives

#### A. Market Objectives

These objectives focus on the product's market penetration and market share acquisition.

1. **Market Share:** Aim to achieve a specific market percentage within a set period.

2. **Geographic Expansion:** Aim to enter new geographic markets or market segments.

3. **Brand Positioning:** Improve brand perception and position the product as a market leader.

#### B. Sales Objectives

These objectives concern the product's sales and revenue generation.

1. **Revenue Target:** Achieve a specific sales volume or revenue within a specific period.

2. **Units Sold:** Sell a specific number of product units.

3. **Profit Margin:** Achieve a desired profit margin through pricing strategies and cost control.

#### C. Product Objectives

These objectives focus on the product's features, functionality, and quality.

1. **Product Innovation:** Introduce new features or improvements to differentiate from competitors.

2. **Product Quality:** Maintain or improve product quality to meet customer expectations.

3. **Development Time:** Reduce the time required for product development and launch.

#### D. Customer Objectives

These objectives aim to improve customer experience and satisfaction.

1. **Customer Satisfaction:** Achieve a specific customer satisfaction score (CSAT).

2. **Customer Loyalty:** Increase customer retention rate and reduce churn rate.

3. **Customer Service:** Improve response times and the quality of customer service.

#### E. Marketing Objectives

These objectives focus on promotional activities and demand generation.

1. **Lead Generation:** Generate a specific number of qualified leads.

2. **Brand Awareness:** Increase brand awareness through marketing campaigns.

3. **Campaign ROI:** Achieve a desired return on investment (ROI) for marketing campaigns.

### 3. Objective Definition Process

#### A. Situational Analysis

Before defining objectives, it is essential to conduct a situational analysis to understand the current context of the product. This includes:

1. **SWOT Analysis:** Assess the product's strengths, weaknesses, opportunities, and threats.

2. **Market Analysis:** Understand market dynamics, trends, and customer needs.

3. **Competitor Analysis:** Study key

competitors and their strategies.

#### B. Stakeholder Involvement

Involving key stakeholders in the objective definition process is crucial for gaining broad consensus and support. This includes:

1. **Product Development Team:** Ensure that objectives are realistic and achievable from a technical standpoint.

2. **Sales and Marketing Team:** Align objectives with sales and marketing capabilities and strategies.

3. **Corporate Leadership:** Ensure that objectives align with the company's vision and strategy.

#### C. SMART Objective Definition

Objectives should be SMART, i.e., Specific,

Measurable, Achievable, Realistic, and Time-bound. This approach ensures that objectives are clear and attainable.

1. **Specific:** Clearly define what you want to achieve.

2. **Measurable:** Establish criteria to measure progress.

3. **Achievable:** Ensure objectives are realistic and attainable.

4. **Realistic:** Consider available resources and capabilities.

5. **Time-bound:** Define a deadline for achieving the objectives.

#### D. Objective Documentation

Clearly and thoroughly documenting objectives is essential for communication and monitoring. Documentation should include:

1. **Objective Description:** Detailed description of what you aim to achieve.

2. **Measurement Metrics:** Define specific metrics that will be used to measure progress.

3. **Responsibility:** Assign specific responsibilities to team members.

4. **Timeline:** Establish a timeline with key milestones and deadlines.

### 4. Monitoring and Evaluating Objectives

#### A. Continuous Monitoring

Continuous monitoring is essential to ensure objectives are on track. This includes:

1. **Regular Reporting:** Create periodic reports to monitor progress against objectives.

2. **Review Meetings:** Organize regular meetings with the team to discuss progress and identify any issues.

#### B. Adaptation and Correction

It is important to be flexible and ready to adapt objectives based on market changes or feedback received. This may include:

1. **Data Analysis:** Use collected data to identify areas for improvement.

2. **Customer Feedback:** Incorporate customer feedback to adapt strategies.

3. **Objective Review:** Review and, if necessary, modify objectives to ensure they are still relevant and achievable.

#### C. Final Evaluation

At the end of the defined period for the objectives, it is essential to conduct a final evaluation to understand if the objectives have been achieved and what can be learned from the experience. This includes:

1. **Performance Evaluation:** Measure the results obtained against the set objectives.

2. **Lessons Learned:** Document lessons learned to improve future processes.

3. **Future Planning:** Use the information gathered to define new objectives and strategies.

### 5. Examples of Product Objectives

#### A. Revenue Objective

- **Description:** Achieve a revenue of 5 million euros by the end of the fiscal year.

- **Measurement Metrics:** Monthly revenue, sales growth rate.

- **Responsibility:** Sales Director, Marketing Team.

- **Timeline:** January 1 to December 31.

#### B. Geographic Expansion Objective

- **Description:** Expand product presence in Asian markets by the second quarter.

- **Measurement Metrics:** Number of new distributors, sales in new markets.

- **Responsibility:** International Operations Manager.

- **Timeline:** January 1 to June 30.

#### C. Product Innovation Objective

- **Description:** Launch a new product version with advanced features by the third quarter.

- **Measurement Metrics:** Number of new features, customer feedback.

- **Responsibility:** Product Development

Team.

- **Timeline:** January 1 to September 30.

#### D. Customer Satisfaction Objective

- **Description:** Increase customer satisfaction score by 20% by the end of the year.

- **Measurement Metrics:** CSAT score, number of customer complaints.

- **Responsibility:** Customer Service Director.

- **Timeline:** January 1 to December 31.

#### E. Lead Generation Objective

- **Description:** Generate 10,000 qualified leads by the first half of the year.

- **Measurement Metrics:** Number of leads generated, lead conversion rate.

- **Responsibility:** Digital Marketing Team.

- **Timeline:** January 1 to June 30.


Defining product objectives is a fundamental process in product marketing that requires a strategic and well-planned approach. Clear, specific, and measurable objectives not only guide product development and launch but also facilitate performance monitoring and evaluation. Involving key stakeholders, using SMART methodologies, and adopting a flexible approach to adapt to changes are essential steps to ensure product success. With accurate objective definition, companies can enhance their competitiveness, meet customer needs, and achieve sustainable growth.

## 4. Developing the Product in Product Marketing

Product development is a complex, multi-phase process that requires careful planning and effective collaboration between various company departments. This process includes creating a product concept, defining the product's features and benefits, and developing a detailed development plan. Let's explore these aspects in detail.

### 1. Creating a Product Concept

The product concept is the basic idea around which the product will be built. It is a clear and concise description of what the product represents, the problem it solves, and how it differentiates from competitors. Creating a solid concept is fundamental to guide all subsequent stages of product development.

#### A. Identifying Market Needs

The first step in creating a product concept is identifying the needs and requirements of the market. This can be done through:

1. **Market Research:** Utilize surveys, interviews, and focus groups to gather data on customer needs.

2. **Trend Analysis:** Study market trends and changes in consumer preferences.

3. **Customer Feedback:** Gather feedback from existing customers to understand their expectations and pain points.

#### B. Brainstorming and Idea Generation

Once market needs are identified, the next step is generating ideas for the new product. This process can include:

1. **Brainstorming Sessions:** Involve

various departments to generate a wide range of ideas.

2. **Competitor Analysis:** Examine competing products to identify gaps and differentiation opportunities.

3. **Creativity and Innovation:** Encourage innovation and creativity to develop unique and original ideas.

#### C. Evaluation and Selection of Ideas

Not all ideas generated will be viable or feasible. Therefore, it is necessary to evaluate and select the most promising ideas. This can be done through:

1. **Feasibility Analysis:** Assess the technical, financial, and commercial feasibility of the ideas.

2. **Prioritization:** Use criteria such as market potential, alignment with company strategy, and differentiation capability to prioritize ideas.

3. **Prototyping and Testing:** Create prototypes of the selected ideas and test them with a group of customers to gather feedback and assess market acceptance.

#### D. Defining the Concept

After selecting the best idea, the next step is to define the product concept. This includes:

1. **Product Description:** A clear and detailed description of the product, including its purpose, main features, and how it solves customer problems.

2. **Value Proposition:** The product's unique value proposition, i.e., the distinctive benefits it offers to customers compared to competitors.

3. **Market Segment:** Identification of the target market and personas (buyer personas) for which the product is intended.

4. **Product Positioning:** How the product will be positioned in the market relative to

competitors.

### 2. Defining the Product Features and Benefits

Once the product concept is defined, it is necessary to detail the specific features of the product and the benefits it offers to customers. This step is crucial for guiding the technical development of the product and for creating effective marketing materials.

#### A. Identifying Key Features

The key features of the product are the attributes or functionalities that define it and make it useful for customers. This process includes:

1. **Feature List:** Create a detailed list of the product's functionalities and technical specifications.

2. **Feature Prioritization:** Prioritize features based on their importance to customers and their market impact.

3. **Technical Documentation:** Create technical documents that detail the product specifications to guide development and production.

#### B. Translating Features into Benefits

Customers do not buy features, but the benefits these features provide. Therefore, it is essential to translate the product features into clear and understandable benefits for customers. This includes:

1. **Identifying Benefits:** Determine how each product feature translates into a tangible benefit for the customer.

2. **Communicating Benefits:** Create marketing messages that highlight the product benefits and resonate with customers' needs and aspirations.

3. **Social Proof:** Use testimonials, case studies, and reviews to demonstrate the product benefits through the experiences of other customers.

#### C. Creating a Feature-Benefit Matrix

A feature-benefit matrix is a useful tool for mapping each product feature to its corresponding benefits. This helps ensure that all product features are clearly linked to customer benefits and facilitates the creation of marketing and sales materials.

### 3. Creating a Product Development Plan

The product development plan is a detailed document that outlines all activities necessary to bring the product from concept to market. This plan includes phases, activities, resources, timelines, and responsibilities.

#### A. Defining Development Phases

The product development process can be divided into several phases, each with specific objectives and activities. The main development phases include:

1. **Ideation and Concept:** Idea generation and selection, product concept definition.

2. **Planning and Design:** Detailed project planning, product design, prototyping.

3. **Development and Testing:** Product development, testing and iteration, resolution of technical issues.

4. **Production and Launch:** Scale production, launch planning, marketing and sales activities.

5. **Post-Launch and Continuous Improvement:** Monitoring product performance, gathering feedback, continuous improvements.

#### B. Detailing Activities

For each phase of the development process, it is necessary to detail the specific activities that need to be completed. This includes:

1. **Design and Engineering:** Creating technical drawings, developing prototypes, feasibility testing.

2. **Testing and Validation:** Functional, usability, and reliability testing, product validation with customers.

3. **Production and Logistics:** Production planning, material procurement, supply chain management.

4. **Marketing and Sales:** Creating marketing materials, launch campaign planning, sales team training.

#### C. Resource Allocation

An effective product development plan requires the allocation of necessary resources. This includes:

1. **Human Resources:** Identifying the teams and skills needed for each project phase.

2. **Financial Resources:** Defining the budget for product development, including R&D, production, marketing, and launch costs.

3. **Technical Resources:** Identifying the tools and technologies required for product development and testing.

#### D. Defining Timelines

The product development plan must include a detailed timeline with key milestones and deadlines. This helps ensure the project stays on schedule and that all activities are completed in a coordinated manner.

1. **Project Timeline:** Create a timeline covering all project phases, from ideation to launch.

2. **Milestones:** Define key milestones to monitor progress and identify any delays.

3. **Time Management:** Use project management tools to track timelines and adjust the plan as needed.

#### E. Monitoring and Control

Monitoring and controlling project progress is essential to ensure the product is developed according to plan and to identify any issues promptly. This includes:

1. **KPI and Metrics:** Define Key Performance Indicators (KPIs) and metrics to monitor project progress and performance.

2. **Regular Reporting:** Create periodic reports to inform stakeholders about project progress.

3. **Risk Management:** Identify and manage project risks to minimize the impact of any issues.

### Examples of Product Development Plans

#### A. Developing a New Smartphone

1. **Ideation and Concept:** Market research, idea generation, product concept definition.

2. **Planning and Design:** Design planning, prototype development, usability testing.

3. **Development and Testing:** Hardware and software development, functionality testing, technical issue resolution.

4. **Production and Launch:** Production planning, material procurement, marketing campaigns.

5. **Post-Launch and Continuous Improvement:** Sales monitoring, feedback collection, software updates.

#### B. Developing SaaS Software

1. **Ideation and Concept:** Identifying market needs, defining the software concept, creating user personas.

2. **Planning and Design:** Feature planning, user interface design, prototype development.

3. **Development and Testing:** Code development, usability and security testing, iteration based on feedback.

4. **Production and Launch:** Infrastructure preparation, pricing plans, market launch.

5. **Post-Launch and Continuous Improvement:** Performance monitoring, continuous updates and improvements, customer support.

Developing a product in the context of product marketing is a strategic, multi-phase process that requires careful planning and effective collaboration between various company departments. Creating a solid product concept, clearly defining product features and benefits, and developing a detailed development plan are essential steps to ensure the product's success in the market. With a methodical approach and effective project management, companies can develop innovative products that meet customer needs and contribute to long-term success.

## 5. Product Positioning in the Market

Product positioning in the market is a crucial element in product marketing, as it determines how a product is perceived by consumers compared to competitors. Effective positioning helps differentiate the product, create a clear and desirable image in the consumers' minds, and guide marketing and sales strategies. This guide explores in detail how to identify the product positioning, define the unique selling proposition (USP), and create an effective positioning strategy.

### 1. Identifying the Product Positioning in the Market

#### A. Market and Customer Analysis

To identify the product positioning, it is essential to understand the market and customers. This process begins with an in-depth market analysis to identify the needs, preferences, and behaviors of consumers.

1. **Market Segmentation:**

   - **Demographic:** Age, gender, income, education.

   - **Geographic:** Region, city, climate.

   - **Psychographic:** Lifestyle, values, personality.

   - **Behavioral:** Buying habits, brand loyalty, product usage.

2. **Customer Analysis:**

   - **Market Research:** Surveys, interviews, focus groups.

   - **Customer Feedback:** Collecting reviews, comments, and suggestions.

   - **Customer Journey:** Mapping the customer journey to understand touchpoints and experiences.

#### B. Competitor Analysis

Knowing the competitors is fundamental to identifying the product positioning. This includes:

1. **Identifying Competitors:**

   - **Direct:** Products that offer similar solutions to customer needs.

   - **Indirect:** Products that satisfy related or alternative needs.

2. **Analyzing Competitors' Strategies:**

   - **Value Proposition:** Evaluating what competitors offer to customers.

   - **Pricing:** Analyzing the pricing strategy.

   - **Distribution Channels:** Studying where and how competitors' products are sold.

   - **Marketing Messages:** Examining key

messages and advertising campaigns.

3. **Benchmarking:**

   - **Product Performance:** Comparing features, quality, and innovation.

   - **Brand Positioning:** Evaluating how competitors are perceived by customers.

#### C. SWOT Analysis

SWOT analysis (Strengths, Weaknesses, Opportunities, Threats) is a useful tool to evaluate the product's market position.

1. **Strengths:** Identifying the features that make the product unique and advantageous.

2. **Weaknesses:** Recognizing areas where the product can improve.

3. **Opportunities:** Identifying market trends and growth areas.

4. **Threats:** Assessing risks and challenges in the market.

### 2. Defining the Unique Selling Proposition (USP)

The unique selling proposition (USP) is the distinctive element that makes the product unique and attractive to customers. An effective USP answers the question: "Why should customers choose our product over the competitors'?"

#### A. Identifying Key Benefits

The key benefits of the product must be clearly identified and communicated. This includes:

1. **Unique Features:** Characteristics that no other product offers.

2. **Superior Quality:** Significant improvements compared to competitors.

3. **Customer Experience:** Benefits related to product usage, such as ease of use or excellent customer support.

4. **Value for Money:** Good quality-price ratio.

#### B. Highlighting Differentiation Points

It is important to highlight the product's differentiation points to make them attractive and relevant to the target market.

1. **Innovation:** Emphasizing innovative aspects and new technologies.

2. **Branding:** Building a strong and recognizable brand identity.

3. **Testimonials and Case Studies:** Using success stories and positive customer feedback.

#### C. Simplicity and Clarity

The USP must be simple and clear, easily understandable by customers.

1. **Concise Messages:** Avoiding technical jargon and using clear and direct language.

2. **Visualization:** Using images and graphics to illustrate benefits.

3. **Emotional Appeal:** Linking the USP to emotional values that resonate with customers.

### 3. Creating an Effective Positioning Strategy

An effective positioning strategy integrates market understanding, the USP, and a clear marketing plan to reach and influence the target customers.

#### A. Defining Positioning Objectives

Establishing clear and measurable objectives for product positioning.

1. **Market Objectives:** Market share percentage to achieve, specific market segments.

2. **Brand Objectives:** Increasing brand awareness, improving brand perception.

3. **Financial Objectives:** Sales growth, profit margin improvement.

#### B. Developing Positioning Messages

Creating positioning messages that clearly communicate the USP and product benefits.

1. **Key Messages:** Developing key messages that reflect the value proposition.

2. **Segment Adaptation:** Customizing messages for different market segments.

3. **Communication Channels:** Selecting the most effective channels to reach the target market, such as social media, email marketing, traditional advertising.

#### C. Implementing the Positioning Strategy

Executing the positioning strategy through marketing campaigns and promotional initiatives.

1. **Product Launch:** Planning and executing a product launch that generates interest and visibility.

2. **Promotions and Offers:** Using promotions, discounts, and special offers to attract customers.

3. **Events and Sponsorships:** Participating in trade shows, industry events, and sponsorships to increase brand visibility.

#### D. Monitoring and Evaluation

Monitoring the effectiveness of the positioning strategy and making necessary adjustments based on results.

1. **Data Analysis:** Using analytics tools to monitor sales, web traffic, and social media engagement.

2. **Customer Feedback:** Collecting and analyzing customer feedback to understand perceptions and improve the product.

3. **Strategy Adaptation:** Making adjustments to the positioning strategy based on collected data and feedback.

### Examples of Product Positioning

#### A. Apple iPhone

1. **Identifying the Positioning:**

   - **Market Segment:** Premium customers seeking advanced technology and elegant design.

   - **Positioning:** Technological innovation and high-quality design.


2. **Unique Selling Proposition (USP):**

   - **Innovation:** Cutting-edge technology, advanced cameras, high performance.

   - **Design:** Elegant aesthetics and high-quality materials.

   - **Ecosystem:** Seamless integration with other Apple products.


3. **Positioning Strategy:**

   - **Positioning Messages:** "Think Different," "The best iPhone ever."

   - **Communication Channels:** TV advertising, social media, Apple stores.

   - **Product Launch:** Spectacular launch

events, online pre-orders.

#### B. Tesla Model S

1. **Identifying the Positioning:**

   - **Market Segment:** Eco-conscious and tech-savvy customers.

   - **Positioning:** Luxury electric car with exceptional performance.

2. **Unique Selling Proposition (USP):**

   - **Technology:** Advanced autopilot, over-the-air software updates.

   - **Performance:** Rapid acceleration, long range.

   - **Sustainability:** Zero emissions, eco-friendly production.

3. **Positioning Strategy:**

   - **Positioning Messages:** "The future of

driving," "Sustainability without compromise."

  - **Communication Channels:** Social media, corporate events, test drives.

  - **Product Launch:** Online marketing campaigns, direct pre-orders, presentation events.

Product positioning in the market is a strategic process that requires a deep understanding of the market, customers, and competitors. Defining a clear and differentiating unique selling proposition (USP) is crucial for attracting and retaining customers. A well-planned and implemented positioning strategy can make the difference between a product's success and failure. With a methodical and data-driven approach, companies can effectively position their products to meet customer needs and gain a sustainable competitive advantage.

# 6. Pricing: Strategies for Analyzing Competition, Setting Sale Prices, and Increasing Sales

Pricing, or setting the sale price, is a crucial component of the marketing mix that can significantly influence a product's market success. Developing an effective pricing strategy requires in-depth competitor analysis, a clear understanding of perceived consumer value, and the implementation of dynamic and adaptive pricing techniques. This guide explores in detail how to analyze the competition, determine the sale price, and create pricing strategies to increase sales.

### 1. Analyzing the Competition

#### A. Identifying Competitors

The first step in analyzing the competition is to identify the main competitors in the market. These can be divided into:

1. **Direct Competitors:** Offer similar products or services and target the same market.

2. **Indirect Competitors:** Offer alternative products or services that meet similar needs.

#### B. Gathering Information on Competitors

Once competitors are identified, it is essential to gather detailed information about them. The primary sources of information include:

1. **Websites and Advertising Materials:** Analyze competitors' websites, brochures, and other advertising materials.

2. **Financial Reports:** Examine annual reports and public financial statements.

3. **Customer Reviews:** Read online reviews and customer feedback on competitors' products.

4. **Market Surveys:** Conduct market surveys to obtain direct information from consumers about competitors.

#### C. Analyzing Competitors' Prices

A critical aspect of competitor analysis is price analysis. This includes:

1. **Price Monitoring:** Collect data on competitors' product prices through websites, physical stores, and e-commerce platforms.

2. **Discount and Promotion Policies:** Analyze competitors' discount policies, seasonal promotions, and special offers.

3. **Price Structures:** Examine how competitors structure their prices, such as offering bundled prices, subscription plans, or tiered pricing.

#### D. Evaluating the Value Offered by Competitors

Evaluating the value offered by competitors relative to their price is essential for understanding their pricing strategy. This can be done through:

1. **Product Feature Analysis:** Compare the features, functionalities, and quality of competitors' products.

2. **Customer Perceived Value:** Use surveys and interviews to understand how customers perceive the value of competitors' products.

3. **Brand Positioning:** Assess how competitors are positioned in the market and how customers perceive their brand.

### 2. Determining the Sale Price

#### A. Pricing Objectives

Determining the sale price begins with

defining the pricing objectives. These may include:

1. **Profit Maximization:** Set a price that maximizes profit margins.

2. **Market Share Increase:** Set a competitive price to increase market share.

3. **Cost Recovery:** Ensure the price covers all production, distribution, and marketing costs.

4. **Brand Valuation:** Use pricing to position the product as premium or luxury.

#### B. Cost Analysis

A fundamental step in determining the sale price is cost analysis. This includes:

1. **Fixed Costs:** Costs that do not vary with production levels, such as rent, salaries, and depreciation.

2. **Variable Costs:** Costs that vary

directly with production levels, such as raw materials, direct labor, and shipping expenses.

3. **Desired Profit Margin:** Determine the desired profit margin to be added to the total costs to set the final price.

#### C. Pricing Methods

There are several pricing methods that can be used to determine the sale price:

1. **Cost-Plus Pricing:** Adding a fixed profit margin to the total product cost.

2. **Competitive Pricing:** Setting the price based on competitors' prices.

3. **Value-Based Pricing:** Setting the price based on the perceived value to the customer.

4. **Dynamic Pricing:** Adjusting prices in real-time based on demand and supply.

#### D. Price Testing

Before launching the product in the market, it is useful to test different pricing options to see which works best. This can include:

1. **A/B Testing:** Offering the product at different prices to similar groups of customers and comparing the results.

2. **Price Experiments:** Conducting price experiments in pilot markets or through online sales channels.

3. **Customer Feedback:** Collecting feedback from customers about their willingness to pay for the product.

### 3. Creating Pricing Strategies to Increase Sales

#### A. Psychological Pricing Strategies

Psychological pricing strategies leverage consumer behavior and perception to encourage sales.

1. **Fractional Pricing:** Use prices that end in .99 or .95 to make the price seem lower (e.g., $19.99 instead of $20.00).

2. **Anchor Pricing:** Display a higher price next to the actual price to make the latter appear as a bargain.

3. **Bundle Pricing:** Offer a package of products at a lower price than the sum of individual product prices.

#### B. Discount and Promotion Strategies

Discount and promotion strategies can increase sales by attracting new customers and encouraging repeat purchases.

1. **Temporary Discounts:** Offer discounts for a limited period to create a sense of urgency.

2. **Loyalty Programs:** Offer discounts and

rewards to loyal customers to encourage repeat purchases.

3. **Cross-Selling Promotions:** Offer discounts on complementary products to increase the average order value.

#### C. Dynamic Pricing Strategies

Dynamic pricing strategies allow prices to be adjusted in real-time based on various factors.

1. **Demand-Based Pricing:** Increase prices when demand is high and lower them when demand is low.

2. **Time-Based Pricing:** Use different prices at different times of the day or week.

3. **Customer Segment Pricing:** Offer different prices to different customer segments based on their willingness to pay.

#### D. Premium Pricing Strategies

Premium pricing strategies can be used to position the product as exclusive and high-quality.

1. **Prestige Pricing:** Set a high price to create an image of luxury and quality.

2. **Limited Edition:** Offer limited editions of the product at a higher price.

3. **Customized Experiences:** Offer customization options at a premium price.

#### E. Monitoring and Adapting the Price

It is essential to constantly monitor the performance of pricing strategies and adapt them based on the results obtained.

1. **Sales Analysis:** Monitor sales to see how customers respond to different prices.

2. **Customer Feedback:** Collect continuous feedback from customers about prices.

3. **Competition:** Monitor changes in competitors' prices and adjust your strategies accordingly.

### Examples of Pricing Strategies

#### A. Example of Aplx (Fictional Name)

1. **Competitor Analysis:**

   - Aplx closely monitors the prices of its main competitors like Samsung and Google.

   - Analyzes the value propositions of competitors, including hardware, software, and services.

2. **Determining the Sale Price:**

   - Aplx uses a premium pricing approach, positioning its products as high-quality and desirable.

   - Considers high production costs and the desired profit margin to set prices.

3. **Pricing Strategies:**

   - **Prestige Pricing:** Aplx maintains high prices to position its products as luxury items.

# 7. Implementing a Product Communication Strategy

Marketing and communication are two fundamental elements for promoting a product or a company. Creating an effective marketing strategy is essential to reach your target audience efficiently and effectively. To achieve this, it is important to consider various aspects, such as product positioning in the market, defining the target audience, planning promotional activities, and evaluating the results.

One of the first steps in creating an effective marketing strategy is conducting a thorough market analysis to understand the context in which you operate and identify existing opportunities and threats. In this context, it is important to also evaluate the competition to understand the strengths and weaknesses of other companies in the market and how you can differentiate yourself from them.

Once the reference context is defined, it is necessary to precisely define your target audience. This means identifying the demographic, socio-economic, and behavioral characteristics of the audience you are targeting, in order to create a targeted and effective advertising message.

After identifying your target audience, it is important to define the product's positioning in the market. Positioning involves differentiating your product from the competition by highlighting its strengths and the reasons why consumers should choose it over other available options. In this context, it is crucial to define a unique and distinctive value proposition that can capture attention and satisfy the needs and desires of the target audience.

Once the product positioning is defined, you can move on to planning promotional activities. These activities can be of various types, such as advertising through traditional media, point-of-sale promotion, direct marketing, relationship marketing, and digital marketing. It is essential to choose the communication channels that are most suitable for your target audience and the characteristics of the product, in order to maximize the impact of promotional activities and achieve greater visibility in the market.

Finally, it is important to evaluate the results of promotional activities to understand if the adopted marketing strategy is effective or if modifications are necessary. In this regard, it is crucial to constantly monitor the performance of promotional activities through data analysis and the use of key performance indicators, which allow you to evaluate the effectiveness of the actions taken and make any necessary adjustments.

In addition to defining an effective marketing strategy, it is crucial to develop marketing and promotional materials that can capture the public's attention and effectively communicate the values and benefits of your product. These materials can be of various types, such as brochures, flyers, advertising banners, print ads, TV spots, social media posts, email marketing, websites, and landing pages. It is essential that these materials are consistent with the adopted marketing strategy and clearly and effectively convey the company's advertising message.

To develop successful marketing and promotional materials, it is important to consider the characteristics of your target audience and the most suitable communication channels to reach them. It is crucial to create advertising messages that are clear, persuasive, and emotional, capable of capturing the public's attention and stimulating interest in the product or service offered by the company. It is also important to choose an attractive design and engaging graphics that can enhance the advertising message and make the marketing materials visually appealing and effective.

Finally, it is crucial to implement a product communication strategy to create a relationship of trust and long-term engagement with your target audience. Communication is a fundamental element to convey the company's values and principles, provide detailed information about the product or service offered, and create a constant dialogue with the public.

To implement an effective communication strategy, it is important to use various communication channels, such as websites, social media, corporate blogs, newsletters, events, and fairs, to reach your target audience effectively. It is essential to create quality and valuable content that can engage the audience and stimulate interest in the product or service offered by the company.

Moreover, it is important to constantly monitor the progress of communication and gather public feedback to evaluate the effectiveness of the activities performed and make any necessary adjustments. It is also crucial to be transparent and authentic in communication, providing clear and truthful information about the product and the company, and establishing an open and sincere dialogue with the public.


Marketing and communication are two fundamental elements for promoting a product or a company. Creating an effective marketing strategy, developing engaging marketing and promotional materials, and implementing an effective communication strategy are essential steps to reach your target audience efficiently and effectively. It is important to constantly monitor the performance of the activities carried out and make any necessary adjustments to maximize the impact of the actions taken and achieve greater visibility in the market.

## 8. Product Planning and Launch

Launching a new product in the market is a crucial moment for any company. It is the moment when months or even years of research, development, and production come to fruition and are presented to the public. Therefore, it is essential to carefully plan the product launch to maximize the chances of success and achieve the best return on investment.

The first phase of product launch planning is defining objectives. It is important to establish the short-term and long-term goals you want to achieve with the product launch. These can include increasing sales, acquiring new customers, gaining market share, or improving brand image. Clearly defining objectives helps guide strategic decisions and assess the success of the launch once it has occurred.

Once the objectives are defined, it is necessary to identify the target audience for the new product. Who are the potential buyers, what are their needs and purchasing motivations, which communication channels do they use, and how do they relate to the brand? This information is crucial to creating an effective launch message and selecting the most suitable distribution channels.

The next phase involves defining the product launch strategy. This strategy must be based on a detailed analysis of the market, competitors, and consumer trends. It is important to understand how the new product positions itself relative to the competition and what are its strengths and weaknesses. This allows identifying opportunities and threats in the market and adopting necessary countermeasures.

A key element of the product launch strategy is defining the positioning. How do you want the new product to be perceived by consumers? What are the values, benefits, and attributes you want to communicate? The product positioning will influence all marketing and communication decisions made for the launch.

In particular, it is crucial to define the product launch message. This message must be clear, memorable, and persuasive, capable of capturing the public's attention and effectively communicating the advantages and distinctive features of the product. The launch message must be consistent with the product positioning and should be repeated across all communication channels used for the launch.

Another important aspect of the product launch strategy is the selection of distribution channels. You need to decide which distribution channels are best suited to reach the target audience and what distribution strategies to adopt. In some cases, it may be appropriate to use traditional channels, such as physical stores or distributors, while in other cases, it may be more effective to use digital channels, such as e-commerce or social media.

Along with the choice of distribution channels, it is also necessary to plan promotional and communication activities for the product launch. These activities can include advertising, public relations, launch events, influencer marketing, social media marketing, and many others. It is important to define an integrated communication plan that involves all available communication channels and effectively reaches the target audience.

An often overlooked aspect of the product launch strategy is managing expectations. It is important to communicate transparently and honestly to consumers what they can expect from the new product and what its real benefits are. It is better to manage customer expectations rather than promise something that the product cannot deliver. The credibility of the brand depends on its ability to keep promises made to consumers.

Finally, it is essential to monitor and evaluate the effectiveness of the product launch once it has occurred. It is important to measure the results obtained against the set objectives and understand the factors that contributed to the success or failure of the launch. Only by critically analyzing the results can you learn from mistakes and improve future strategies.

Launching a new product in the market is an exciting yet challenging moment for any company. Carefully planning the product launch, creating an effective strategy, and constantly monitoring results are the keys to maximizing the chances of success and achieving the best return on investment.

## 9. Monitoring and evaluating launch results

Monitoring and evaluating the results of a product launch in product marketing is a critical phase of the market launch process. This phase is essential to understand whether the set objectives have been achieved and whether the launch strategy has been successful or if there are areas that need improvement.

Monitoring the launch results involves analyzing a series of key performance indicators (KPIs) that allow evaluating the product's impact on the market. These KPIs may include sales numbers, market share acquired, conversion rate, return on investment (ROI), customer satisfaction level, product awareness, and many other factors that can vary depending on the launch objective and industry.

One of the first steps in monitoring launch results is establishing the KPIs to monitor and defining how they will be measured. For example, if the launch goal is to increase sales, it will be necessary to monitor the number of units sold, revenue generated from the launched product, and market share acquired compared to competitors. If the goal is to increase product awareness, it will be important to monitor website visits, growth of social media followers, number of articles published in specialized press, etc.

Once the KPIs are defined and measurement methods established, it is important to have the technological means and human resources necessary to collect data in real time or as close as possible to the event being monitored. Tools such as Google Analytics, CRM platforms, social media monitoring software, surveys, and market research can be used to gather information and track launch results.

After collecting the data, it is important to analyze it to understand whether the set objectives have been achieved and if there are any issues or areas for improvement. For example, if the number of units sold is below expectations, it may be necessary to review pricing strategy, marketing communication, or product positioning in the market. If the acquired market share is growing, it may instead be necessary to invest more in marketing and communication to consolidate success and increase brand perception.

Another important aspect to consider in evaluating launch results is analyzing customer and user feedback. Customer reviews and comments on social media, e-commerce platforms, or industry forums can provide valuable insights into product perception, strengths and weaknesses, areas for improvement, and unmet expectations. It is important to carefully evaluate this feedback and use it to make any necessary changes to the product or marketing strategy.

Finally, it is important to continuously monitor launch results over time to assess the product's evolution in the market and its long-term impact. This can be achieved through constant monitoring of KPIs and updating marketing strategies based on the results obtained. Additionally, it is important to be flexible and ready to modify marketing and launch strategies based on new market trends, customer needs, and competitor actions.

In conclusion, monitoring and evaluating the results of a product launch in product marketing is a crucial phase of the market launch process that allows measuring the effectiveness of the marketing strategy, evaluating the product's performance in the market, and making any necessary changes to improve performance and achieve set objectives. It is important to use a combination of KPIs, technological tools, and analysis of customer feedback to effectively monitor results and ensure the success of the market launch.

## 10. Distribution Channels

In the field of Product Marketing, managing distribution channels is crucial to ensuring the success of a product in the market. Identifying the most suitable distribution channels and managing them effectively can make the difference between success and failure of a product.

When we talk about distribution channels, we refer to the paths through which a product passes before reaching the end consumer. These channels can be physical, such as traditional stores, or digital, such as e-commerce platforms. It is important to identify the distribution channels most appropriate for your product, taking into account various factors such as target market, product type, competition, and industry trends.

Proper identification of distribution channels allows reaching your target market effectively, ensuring greater visibility and consequently higher sales. It is also important to consider the costs and profit margins associated with each distribution channel to maximize return on investment.

Once the most suitable distribution channels are identified, it is essential to manage them efficiently. This involves good planning and coordination of activities related to product distribution, from production to delivery to the end consumer. Only through proper management of distribution channels can logistical problems, delivery delays, and resource waste be avoided.

Collaboration with retailers and partners is a key aspect of distribution channel management. Working synergistically with retailers and partners allows achieving broader market coverage and expanding your distribution network. It is important to establish strong and lasting relationships with collaborators based on trust, transparency, and reciprocity.

Retailers are a crucial link between the company and the end consumer. Collaborating with reliable and competent retailers helps get your product onto more shelves and increases brand visibility. Supporting retailers with targeted marketing and promotion strategies ensures proper product exposure and stimulates sales.

Strategic partners can also be valuable allies in product distribution. Partners may include other companies in the industry, influencers, bloggers, or specialized publications that can help promote the product and increase its visibility. It is important to carefully select partners based on their reputation, influence, and alignment with the brand's values.

Managing distribution channels therefore requires a well-defined strategy and constant monitoring of performance. It is important to regularly evaluate the effectiveness of the distribution channels used and make any necessary corrections or improvements based on the results obtained. Only through careful management of distribution channels can sales opportunities be maximized and product success in the market be ensured.

Identifying the most suitable distribution channels, effectively managing these channels, and collaborating with retailers and partners are essential for the success of a product in the market. Only through a well-defined strategy and meticulous attention to detail can sales opportunities be maximized and the brand's presence in the market be affirmed.

# 11. Selection of Affordable and High-Quality Items in Product Marketing

In the context of product marketing, the choice of affordable and high-quality items is crucial for the success of a product in the market. This approach aims to meet consumer needs by offering products that combine affordable pricing with high-quality standards. In this guide, we will explore in detail the importance of this strategy, the basic principles for item selection, and some practical examples of effective implementation in the context of product marketing.

### 1. Importance of Selection of Affordable and High-Quality Items

#### A. Customer Satisfaction

Offering affordable and high-quality items is essential to meet customer expectations and enhance their overall product experience. When consumers find value in the price-quality ratio offered, they are more likely to become loyal to the brand and recommend it to others.

#### B. Competitive Advantage

In today's competitive market, differentiation through product quality is an effective way to gain a competitive advantage. Items that combine good quality with affordable pricing can attract customers seeking the best value for money available.

#### C. Consumer Trust

Product quality is closely tied to consumer trust in the brand. Offering items that maintain promised standards helps build and maintain a reputation for reliability and integrity.

#### D. Reduction in Service Costs and Returns

High-quality products tend to be more reliable and less prone to operational issues or defects. This can reduce costs associated with handling returns and customer complaints, thereby improving overall operational efficiency.

#### E. Sustainability

High-quality items are often designed to last longer, thus reducing the environmental impact associated with production and disposal of low-quality products. Promoting sustainability through the production of durable items is a winning strategy in today's social and environmental landscape.

### 2. Basic Principles for Item Selection

#### A. In-Depth Market Research

Selecting affordable and high-quality items begins with in-depth market research to understand consumer needs and preferences. This process includes:

1. **Market Segmentation:** Identifying different customer segments and their specific needs.

2. **Competitive Analysis:** Evaluating products offered by competitors to identify market gaps and untapped opportunities.

3. **Customer Feedback:** Collecting and analyzing customer opinions through surveys, interviews, and online reviews to understand their expectations regarding quality and price.

#### B. Quality Standards

Establishing clear quality standards is crucial to ensure that items meet customer expectations and maintain brand integrity. This includes:

1. **Materials and Production Processes:** Using high-quality materials and rigorous production processes to ensure product durability and reliability.

2. **Quality Control:** Implementing quality control procedures to monitor and ensure compliance with established standards throughout the product lifecycle.

3. **Certifications and Regulations:** Ensuring that items meet applicable safety and quality regulations in the industry and target market.

#### C. Price-Quality Optimization

Finding the right balance between quality and price is crucial to maximize perceived value for customers. This may involve:

1. **Cost Analysis:** Determining production, distribution, and marketing costs to establish a price that covers costs and ensures adequate profit margins.

2. **Price Benchmarking:** Comparing prices of similar products in the market to identify the appropriate and competitive price range.

3. **Pricing Strategies:** Using pricing techniques such as psychological pricing, dynamic pricing, or bundling to optimize perceived value for customers.

#### D. Product Lifecycle

Considering the product lifecycle is essential

in item selection. This includes:

1. **Introduction:** Launching new products with quality that meets customer expectations and pricing that reflects brand value.

2. **Growth:** Expanding the offering of successful products while maintaining quality standards and adjusting prices based on market demand.

3. **Maturity:** Optimizing production processes and reducing costs to maintain price competitiveness without compromising quality.

4. **Decline:** Managing product decline with pricing strategies that may include discounts and liquidations to efficiently clear inventory.

### 3. Practical Examples of Implementation

#### A. IK (fictional name)

1. **Market Research:** IK conducts extensive research to understand customer needs and market trends in the furniture and home furnishings sector.

2. **Quality Standards:** Uses sustainable materials and efficient production processes to offer durable and affordable furniture and home goods.

3. **Price-Quality Optimization:** IK offers a wide range of products at affordable prices without compromising quality, using flat-packaging and self-service strategies to reduce operational costs.

#### B. Uniqlo

1. **Market Research:** Uniqlo studies global consumer preferences for fashion and

apparel through market research and fashion trend analysis.

2. **Quality Standards:** Uses high-quality materials and collaborates with reliable suppliers to ensure its products are comfortable, functional, and stylish.

3. **Price-Quality Optimization:** Uniqlo maintains affordable prices without compromising style or quality of its garments, using efficient production and global distribution strategies.

#### C. XiX (fictional name)

1. **Market Research:** XiX analyzes consumer needs and preferences in the technology and electronics sector through market research and customer feedback.

2. **Quality Standards:** Uses advanced

technologies and collaborates with high-quality suppliers to produce smartphones, smart devices, and other innovative technology products.

3. **Price-Quality Optimization:** XiX offers technologically advanced products at competitive prices, using online sales, direct-to-consumer sales, and minimal advertising investments.

Choosing affordable and high-quality items in product marketing is crucial for building sustainable competitive advantage, satisfying customers, and enhancing brand image. Through thorough market research, application of high-quality standards, optimization of price-quality ratios, and effective product lifecycle strategies, companies can develop a product assortment that effectively meets consumer needs and stands out in the global market. By adopting a customer-centric and innovative approach, companies can ensure continuous success and sustainable long-term growth.

## 12. Product Marketing Strategies

Product marketing is a fundamental part of business strategy, focusing on effectively positioning the product in the market and maximizing its success. To succeed in product marketing, well-studied and targeted strategies are needed to attract consumers and increase sales. Below, I will list 40 effective strategies in product marketing.

1. Know the target audience: First and foremost, understanding the target audience thoroughly—namely, who the potential buyers of the product are and what their needs and preferences are—is crucial.

2. Analyze the competition: It's important to study the competition to understand how to uniquely and distinctly position your product.

3. Define product positioning: Once consumer needs are understood and the competition

analyzed, defining the product's positioning in the market is necessary, communicating its unique and differential values.

4. Create a marketing plan: Develop a detailed marketing plan that includes communication, promotion, and distribution strategies for the product.

5. Develop a strong brand identity: A strong and recognizable brand identity is essential to differentiate from the competition and create an emotional connection with consumers.

6. Use appropriate distribution channels: It's important to choose distribution channels that are most suitable for your product and target audience to maximize visibility and product distribution.

7. Implement a pricing strategy: Pricing is a key element of product marketing and must be carefully calibrated based on product

positioning and competition.

8. Create an integrated communication strategy: Utilize a variety of communication channels, including advertising, social media, PR, and content marketing, to effectively reach consumers.

9. Use influencer marketing: Collaborating with influential influencers and bloggers can help increase product visibility and attract new customers.

10. Harness the power of reviews and testimonials: Positive reviews and testimonials from satisfied customers can be powerful marketing tools to increase consumer trust in the product.

11. Create creative and engaging advertising campaigns: Advertising campaigns must be creative, original, and engaging to capture consumer attention and differentiate the

product from others.

12. Develop strategic partnerships: Collaborating with other companies or complementary brands can help expand product visibility and increase credibility.

13. Offer promotions and discounts: Promotions, discounts, and special offers can incentivize product purchases and attract new customers.

14. Organize launch events and exhibitions: Launch events and exhibitions can generate interest in the product and help highlight its distinctive features.

15. Use content marketing: Creating quality and informative content about the product can help position it as a valuable option for consumers.

16. Implement SEO and SEM strategies: Optimizing the website and product pages for search engines and implementing paid advertising campaigns can improve the product's online visibility.

17. Use remarketing and retargeting: Using remarketing and retargeting to reach customers who have already shown interest in the product and encourage them to make a purchase.

18. Create user-generated content: Involving customers in the marketing process, such as through product photos and reviews, can help generate trust and authenticity around the brand.

19. Constantly monitor performance: It's crucial to constantly monitor the product's performance and marketing strategies to make adjustments and optimizations.

20. Use data analysis tools: Data analysis is essential for understanding consumer behavior and continuously improving marketing strategies.

21. Personalize the customer experience: Offering a personalized experience to customers, such as product recommendations based on their interests, can increase loyalty and customer satisfaction.

22. Implement upselling and cross-selling strategies: Using upselling and cross-selling strategies to increase average order value and maximize revenue.

23. Invest in customer service: Excellent customer service can make a difference in promoting the product and ensuring customer satisfaction.

24. Develop a loyalty marketing strategy: Retaining loyal customers through loyalty

programs and special offers can help maintain brand loyalty and support.

25. Use viral marketing: Harnessing the power of word-of-mouth and viral marketing to increase product visibility and reach a wide audience.

26. Leverage digital marketing trends: Stay updated on the latest digital marketing trends and use them to promote the product innovatively.

27. Launch seasonal promotional campaigns: Utilize holidays and special occasions to launch seasonal promotional campaigns and increase sales.

28. Collaborate with local influencers: Collaborating with local influencers can help reach a specific local audience and increase product visibility in your geographic area.

29. Optimize website user experience: Ensuring that the website is user-friendly and optimized for mobile devices can improve the customer experience and increase conversions.

30. Create partnerships with non-profit organizations: Collaborating with non-profit organizations for charitable purposes can be an opportunity to promote the product and support an important cause.

31. Use networking events: Participating in networking events and trade fairs can help create connections with potential customers and business partners.

32. Implement marketing automation strategies: Use marketing automation tools to automate marketing processes such as email marketing and lead generation.

33. Use user-generated content: Encouraging customers to create user-generated content, such as reviews and photos, can help create an authentic experience for other potential customers.

34. Develop a social media marketing strategy: Use social media to promote the product, engage customers, and create a community around the brand.

35. Promote product eco-sustainability: Communicating the eco-sustainability of the product can attract environmentally-conscious consumers and enhance brand value.

36. Implement referral marketing programs: Create referral marketing programs to incentivize existing customers to bring in new customers and grow the customer base.

37. Use offline marketing: Do not overlook offline marketing opportunities, such as advertisements, brochures, and sponsorships, to reach a broader audience.

38. Develop partnerships with micro-niche influencers: Collaborating with influencers who have a specific niche following can help reach a highly targeted and quality audience.

39. Create evergreen content: Creating evergreen content, i.e., timeless and always relevant content, can help maintain a consistent online presence and attract long-term traffic.

40. Continuously measure and optimize performance: Constantly monitor the performance of marketing strategies, measure results, and continuously make improvements to maximize product marketing success.

Product Marketing is a complex discipline that requires strategic and creative skills to effectively position the product in the market and reach consumers in a targeted manner. Employing these 40 effective strategies in Product Marketing can help maximize product success and establish a strong market presence.

**Index**

1. Introduction pg.4

2. Identifying the Target Market pg.9

3. Define Product Objectives in Product Marketing pg.21

4. Developing the Product in Product Marketing pg.35

5. Product Positioning in the Market pg.49

6. Pricing: Strategies for Analyzing Competition, Setting Sale Prices, and Increasing Sales pg.62

**7. Implementing a Product Communication Strategy pg.74**

**8. Product Planning and Launch pg.80**

**9. Monitoring and evaluating launch results pg.85**

**10. Distribution Channels pg.89**

**11. Selection of Affordable and High-Quality Items in Product Marketing pg.93**

**12. Product Marketing Strategies pg.104**

www.ingramcontent.com/pod-product-compliance
Lightning Source LLC
Chambersburg PA
CBHW071935210526
45479CB00002B/691